organ music

bpNichol

The eroteme in this autobiographical project hovers in an erotics of refusal, an ambiguous, or at most interim, answering to life's and writing's question, "who could resist…" Or, in his acute desire to sustain the wonder, "How do you do? That?" — Fred Wah

organ music
parts of an autobiography
bpNichol

Black Moss Press

Copyright © 2012 Estate of bpNichol

Library and Archives Canada Cataloguing in Publication

Nichol, B. P., 1944-1988
    Organ music : parts of an autobiography /   bpNichol.

ISBN 978-0-88753-515-4

1. Nichol, B. P., 1944-1988--Poetry. I. Title.

PS8527.I32Z53 2012   C811'.54   C2012-904089-4

Cover photo and images on title page, pages 22, 32, 63 and 64 by Andy Phillips
All other photos care of the estate of bpNichol

Layout & design: Kate Hargreaves

Published by Black Moss Press at 2450 Byng Road, Windsor, Ontario, N8W 3E8 Canada. Black Moss books are distributed in Canada and the U.S. by LitDistCo. All orders should be directed there.

Black Moss Press books can also be found on our website www.blackmosspress.com.

Black Moss would like to acknowledge the generous financial support from both the Canada Council of the Arts and the Ontario Arts Council.

PRINTED IN CANADA

for Deanna

who shares the Workman hips
and the rest of the legacy

Some Words of Introduction

I've been working on and at *Organ Music* for some eight years now. The basic idea was to come at the issue of autobiography from another direction i.e. through anecdotes which had their origin in the various parts of the body. I wrote the first one, 'The Vagina,' in March of 1980, and the form it took has been the pattern for all the ones that've followed. As befits an autobiography, all stories are true. They are told in a specific style borrowed from the oral story-telling methods of my Grandma Workman (Leigh) and her brothers & sisters. From a technical standpoint these are the least forgiving pieces I have ever written, by which I mean that unless I get the rhythm of the first few sentences absolutely right the pieces stop dead in their tracks and won't continue until I've corrected whatever the problem is. Which explains why some 8 years of writing had yielded only 11 texts. When

Marty Gervais approached me about publishing *Organ Music* as a book I told him the work wasn't finished. But who knows how long it will take me to finish the rest? I'm not even sure how many the 'rest' are. For some reason the number twenty keeps flashing before my eyes. So I've decided to gather them together into this collection, a kind of interim autobiography as it were. There's more I could add but I'll leave the rest to you. I know most of the parts you'll read about in here aren't organs but who could resist a title like *Organ Music*? Not me.

bpNichol

Contents

The Vagina	11
The Mouth	15
The Tonsils	19
The Chest	23
The Lungs: A Draft	27
The Fingers	33
The Hips	41
The Anus	47
The Toes	51
The Lily	55
Sum of the Parts	59

The Vagina

1.
I never had one.

2.
I lived inside a woman for nine months & inside this male shell all of my life. I floated around on that side of the wall poking & kicking her not looking for exits till I needed them. There came a time I needed you vagina to get thru into this world. First thing I say at the light of day is 'waaah,' Ma.

3.
I thot they all were hairless even tho I bathed with my mother I thot they all were like the little girl's who

came naked to the door I delivered the paper to when I was nine even tho I read the typed porno stories my brother brought back from the navy when I was ten I thot they all were hairless like the nude women's in the sunbathing magazines in the pool hall in Port Arthur even tho I had to know different somewhere I thot they all were hairless & they weren't.

4.
I always wanted one. I grew up wanting one. I thot cocks were okay but vaginas were really nifty. I liked that name for them because it began with 'v' and went 'g' in the middle. I never heard my mother or my sister mention them by name. They were an unspoken mouth & that was the mouth where real things were born. So I came out of that mouth with my mouth flapping 'waaah.' Oh I said that. I said that. I said 'waaah' Ma again & again after I was born.

5.
When I was eleven this kid I knew took me to the drugstore where he worked & showed me some sanitary napkins for men. He said, 'you wear these when you get your period.' I remember he pointed the box out to me & it was way up in the back of this unlit top shelf. I figured I must have some kind of vestigal vagina which was bound to open. I waited almost two years. I never had one.

6.
When sex happened I realized it was all a matter of muscles. I liked the way her muscles worked. She liked the way my muscle worked. It wasn't the one thing or the other thing but the way the two of them worked together. And that was where all the power & the feelings sprang from—the muscles. Alive alive oh.

7.
Doorway. Frame. Mouth. Opening. Passage. The trick is to get from there to here thru her. Or the way Ellie misread that sign on the highway for years: RIGHT LANE MUST EXIST. And of course its the old conundrum—the exit's the entrance. Exit Ma & I exist. And when I fell in love with Ellie I was entranced. Into a world. The world. This world. Our world. Worlds.

The Mouth

1.
You were never supposed to talk when it was full. It was better to keep it shut if you had nothing to say. You were never supposed to shoot it off. It was better to be seen than heard. It got washed out with soap if you talked dirty. You were never supposed to mouth-off, give them any of your lip, turn up your nose at them, give them a dirty look, an evil eye or a baleful stare. So your mouth just sat there, in the middle of your still face, one more set of muscles trying not to give too much away. 'Hey! SMILE! what's the matter with you anyway?'

2.
Probably there are all sorts of stories. Probably my mouth figures in all sorts of stories when I was little but

I don't remember any of them. I don't remember any stories about my mouth but I remember it was there. I remember it was there and I talked & sang & ate & used it all the time. I don't remember anything about it but the mouth remembers. The mouth remembers what the brain can't quite wrap its tongue around & that's what my life's become. My life's become my mouth's remembering, telling stories with the brain's tongue.

3.
I must have been nine. I'm pretty sure I was nine because I remember I was the new boy in school. I remember I was walking on my way there, the back way, thru the woods, & here was this kid walking towards me, George was his name, & I said 'hi George' & he said 'I don't like your mouth' & grabbed me & smashed my face into his knee. It was my first encounter with body art or it was my first encounter with someone else's idea of cosmetic surgery. It was translation or composition. He rearranged me.

4.
The first dentist called me the Cavity Kid & put 35 fillings into me. The second dentist said the first dentist was a charlatan, that all the fillings had fallen out, & put 38 more fillings in me. The third dentist had the shakes from his years in the prisoner of war

camp & called me his 'juicy one,' saliva frothing from my mouth and his shakey hand approached me. The fourth dentist never looked at me. His nurse put me out with the sleeping gas & then he'd enter the room & fill me. The fifth dentist said my teeth were okay but my gums would have to go, he'd have to cut me. The sixth dentist said well he figured an operation on the foot was okay coz the foot was a long way away but the mouth was just a little close to where he thot he lived & boy did we ever agree because I'd begun to see that every time I thot of dentists I ended the sentence with the word 'me.' My mouth was me. I wasn't any ancient Egyptian who believed his Ka was in his nose—nosiree—I was just a Kanadian Kid & had my heart in my mouth every time a dentist approached me.

5.
It all begins with the mouth. I shouted waaa when I was born, maaa when I could name her, took her nipple in, the rubber nipple of the bottle later, the silver spoon, mashed peas, dirt, ants, anything with flavour I could shove there, took the tongue & flung it 'round the mouth making sounds, words, sentences, tried to say the things that made it possible to reach him, kiss her, get my tongue from my mouth into some other. I liked that, liked the fact the tongue could move in mouths other than its own, & that so many things began there—words did, meals, sex—& tho later you

travelled down the body, below the belt, up there you could belt out a duet, share a belt of whisky, undo your belts & put your mouths together. And I like the fact that we are rhymed, mouth to mouth, & that it begins here, on the tongue, in the pun, comes from mouth her mouth where we all come from.

6.
I always said I was part of the oral tradition. I always said poetry was an oral art. When I went into therapy my therapist always said I had an oral personality. I got fixated on oral sex, oral gratification & notating the oral reality of the poem. At the age of five when Al Watts Jr was still my friend I actually said, when asked who could do something or other, 'me or Al' & only years later realized how the truth's flung out of you at certain points & runs on ahead. And here I've been for years running after me, trying to catch up, shouting 'it's the oral,' 'it all depends on the oral,' everybody looking at my bibliography, the too many books & pamphlets, saying with painful accuracy: 'that bp—he really runs off at the mouth.'

The Tonsils

1.
They said 'you don't need them' but they were keen to cut them out. They said 'if they swell up they'll choke you to death' so you learned they cut things off if they might swell up. There were two of them in their sacs & they hung there in your throat. They cut them off.

2.
I didn't have them long enough to grow attached to them but they were attached to me. It was my first real lesson in having no choice. It was my only time ever in a hospital as a kid & I wasn't even sick. I wasn't even sick but I had the operation. I had the operation that I didn't want & I didn't say 'no' because there was no choice really. I had everybody who was bigger than

me telling me this thing was going to happen & me crying a lot & them telling me it was good for me. It was my first real lesson in having no attachments.

3.
Almost everyone I knew had their tonsils out. Almost everyone I knew was told 'it's good for you.' Even tho none of us who had our tonsils out ever knew any kid who choked to death from having them in, almost everyone we knew had their tonsils out.

4.
I miss my tonsils. I think my throat used to feel fuller. Now my throat feels empty a lot & maybe that's why I eat too fast filling the throat with as much as I can. Except food is no substitute for tonsils. The throat just gets empty again.

5.
I was told I didn't need my tonsils. Maybe this is the way it is. Maybe as you grow older they tell you there are other bits you don't need & they cut them out. Maybe they just like cutting them out. Maybe tonsils are a delicacy doctors eat & the younger they are the sweeter. Maybe this is just paranoia. I bet if I had a lobotomy they could cut this paranoia out.

6.
What cutting remarks! What rapier wit! What telling thrusts! Ah cut it out! Cut it short! He can't cut it! You said a mouthful!

7.
There are two of them & they hang there in your throat. There are two of them in sacs & they swell up. Now there are none. Gosh these words seem empty!

The Chest

1.
You were obsessed with it. Everyone was obsessed with it. On the edge of thirteen when Carol Wisdom's chest started to develop you couldn't take your eyes off it. Until you were twelve everyone who was your age had a chest. But then you turned thirteen & you had a chest & she had breasts on her chest & your chest was puny & he really had a chest & she was chesty & all the bad puns began about being 'chest friends' & it was 'chest too much' or 'two much' or 'two for tea anytime baby' (which of course you always said to a guy coz you were too embarrassed to say it to a girl) & suddenly you had discovered chests as if they had never been there before & they were everywhere, everywhere, & you were obsessed with them.

2.
From the age of five to the age of sixteen you kept getting chest colds. Once a year for three weeks you'd be sick in bed, your voice getting deeper (which you liked), your breathing shallower (which you hated), your nostrils redder, your face whiter, saying mutter for mother muttering for her. She'd bring you gingerale (to soothe your throat), vicks vaporub (to clear your head), & you'd say 'I'm gedding bedder' over & over again like a charm clutched to your hopeless chest, 'I'm gedding bedder' you'd say, sinking further into the sheets, 'I'm gedding bedder,' till the bed & you were one pale continuous tone, white on white in white, 'I'm gedding bedder—bedder.'

3.
It was where longing resided. It was what you played your cards close to. It was one of the few body parts rhymed with the furniture & it held hope or tea or linen. It was a clear noun, substantial, the only named part that didn't seem small, didn't seem somehow smaller thru naming. It had no funny names or corny names or dirty names & it was the largest part of all. You stuck it out. You puffed it up. It was chest. What it was was chest.

4.
You didn't think of the chest as sensitive until you danced with her. You were thirteen & the dance floor was crowded & tho the moving bodies of your friends pressed you together you would only allow your chests to touch & there was heat & pressure & movement between you & your chest was ten times more sensitive than your hands, felt more than your eyes could see, & your trapped heart pounded as if you would die, explode, right there before her eyes, disintegrate from the ache & longing. You were in love, your chests were in love, as the music & the crowd carried you, pressing you closer & closer together, over that moving dance floor that dark warm August night.

5.
When you went into therapy all the language changed. Now the chest was something you got things off of or bared, some place you shouldn't keep things inside of, as if it were a vessel & feelings held there grew stagnant, festered, expanded under pressure until released to air. In the shakey diagramming of the unconscious it was where deep lay— deep feelings, deep disturbance—or you thot it was because weren't you always being told you shouldn't be too heady, shouldn't talk off the top of your head, that it was bad to be cut off at the neck, dead from the neck down, & from the neck down is where the chest is. But not too far down because after all you weren't supposed

to dump shit on anyone either, or talk a load of crap, piss on them, be a shit, & what was left then but the chest unless, of course, you had a gut feeling. But gut was too ambiguous, too subject to the charge you were just spewing vomit. No. It was the chest. It had to be the chest; that was where the heart was & the heart was good. You were good-hearted, had a lot of heart &, when you got right down to things you had a heart to heart, really opened up, bared your chest & spoke from your heart all your real feelings, your deep feelings, got everything off your chest, just like you were supposed to.

The Lungs: A Draft
for Robert Kroetsch

1.
This is a breath line. I said. This is a breathline. Line up, he said. Suck your stomach in Nichol, I don't want to see you breathe. I didn't breathe. This was a no breath line. He said. Six or eight or ten of us not breathing while he walked down the line, holding our breath while he looked us over, while he chose one of us to punch in the gut, to see how tough our stomach muscles were he said, stomachs pulled in, lungs pushed out, waiting while he paced back and forth, while he paused in front of each of us and then moved on, this small smile playing across his lips. Waiting. A breathless line. I said.

2.
I was staying at Bob and Smaro's place in Winnipeg. I was sleeping on the floor in Smaro's study. I was getting up early in the morning, like I tend to do, getting up early and going into the livingroom. I was sitting down in a chair and reading a copy of a new book on literary theory or literary criticism Smaro had brought back from some recent trip as she tends to do. I was just turning the page, just beginning to get into the book when Bob appeared at the top of the stairs, when Bob came down the stairs from the upper floor, not really awake, came down the stairs anyway, Bob, muttering to himself, 'life, the great tyrant that makes you go on breathing.' And I thought about breathing. I thought about life. I thought about those great tyrants the lungs, about the lung poems Bob's written, written about, lung forms. And I thought about the lungs sitting there, inside the chest—inhaling—exhaling. And I thought to myself, to myself because Bob was in no mood to hear it, I thought 'life's about going the lung distance.' Just that. And it is.

3.
We were maybe five, Al Watts Jr and me, no more than five, and we had snuck out back, behind the garage, to try a smoke. It was just the way you read it in all those nostalgic memoirs of male childhood. It was authentic. It was a prairie day in Winnipeg in the late '40s and there we were, two buddies sharing

a furtive puff on a stolen cigarette. And just like in all the other stories the father showed up, Al Watts Sr, suddenly appeared around the corner of the garage and said 'so you boys want to smoke, eh?' If only we'd read the stories. If only we'd had the stories read to us. We'd have known then how the whole thing had to end, we'd have known what part the dad plays in these kinds of tales. But we hadn't. We didn't. We said yes we really did want to smoke. And we did. Al Watts Sr took us home, took us back to his study, the room he seldom took us into, and opened up his box of cigars and offered one to each of us. We should have known. We really should have known when he lit them for us and told us to really suck in, to take that smoke right down into our lungs, we should have known what was coming. We didn't. We did it just the way he said. We sucked that smoke right in, right down to our lungs, and of course we started hacking, of course we started coughing, trying to fling the cigars away. But he made us take another smoke, he made us take another three or four good drags on the cigar, until our bodies were racked from the coughing, until our lungs ached from the lunge and heave of trying to push the smoke out. And we didn't want to smoke anymore, I didn't want to smoke anymore, I never really wanted to touch a cigarette again. Even when I was a teenager and hanging out with Easter Egg on his old scow down in Coal Harbour and he'd offer me a toke, I never could take the smoke into my lungs again. Except that after I turned 30 I started smoking cigars. And even though

I didn't take the smoke into my lungs, even though I just held it there in the mouth and let it go, when I thought about it it really didn't make much sense. It didn't you know. Look what had happened to me with Al Watts Sr and Al Watts Jr those many many years ago. This wasn't supposed to be the outcome. This wasn't supposed to be the way the story goes. But it was as if the lungs wanted me to do it. As if the lungs had a memory all their own and I was forced to relive it. Not a primal scream but a primal puff, primal smoke from a primal prairie fire. As if the whole childhood episode had been like one of those moral tales where the reader takes a different lesson from the one the writer intended. Or like one of those shaggy dog jokes, where the punch line comes way after the joke should have ended, way after the person listening had lost all interest in what's being said. Lung time. Different from the head's.

4.
When do you first think of your lungs? When you're young and tiny and turning blue and you can't get your breath because something is happening to you like my mom told me it happened to me? When you're five and choking over your first smoke like I just told you? When you start to sing in the choir and the choirmaster tells you to really fill your lungs with air, your stomach, and support the sound from down there, inside the body? When you take up running, gasp for that last

breath hoping to bring the tape nearer, the finish line, hoping the lungs will hold for the final lunge? Do you think of them then? In a moment like this, trying to remember, can you even say 'I remember this about my lungs'? No. No. Almost no memories at all. Only the notion that they're pumping away, just beneath the surface of these lines, however much these lines do or don't acknowledge them. One of those parts you can't do without. Two of them. 'The bellows,' he bellows, airing his opinion. Because to air is human. To forgive the divine. Bellowing our prays, our songs. Bellowing our lung-ings.

5.
A draft he calls it. Like it blew in through a crack in the mind. Just a bunch of hot air. As when you're really hot, get the cadences to fall, the syllables to trot past the eye and ear just the way you see and hear them in the mind. As tho the mind tapped the lung and each thot hung there in its proper place. 'Its just a draft. I'll get it right later.' He feels the breath heave. He hears the words start as the heart pumps and the lungs take all that air and squeeze it in there, into the blood stream flows thru the mind. No next time when the lungs stop. Like that last sentence on the tongue, hangs in the air after the lungs have pressed their last square inch of it out in the absolute moment of death, only the body left: 'I'll get it right next time.'

The Fingers
for Mary Griffin

1.
There were ten of them. Or were there eight? Everyone always said the thumbs were different. They made you human. They let you know you weren't a great ape. Even tho his sister told him they'd found him in the zoo, a forlorn hairless little monkey the other monkeys had rejected, that ma had taken pity on him and brought him home with them, he knew he was human. He flexed his eight fingers and his two thumbs and he knew he was human. Even when the three year old from next door his sister had taught to call him 'monkey' came in and called him 'monkey' in front of all those guests at the dinner table, he knew. He flexed his fingers. He twiddled his thumbs. 'I'm human,' he said and he knew.

2.
In all the early photos he is holding his sister's hand, his fingers wrapped around her fingers, grabbing hold, hanging on. He is doing this in photo after photo, the left hand usually, the left fingers, while the right hand hangs at his side or pushes his brother away as his brother attempts to hold his hand, pushes his brother away with his right fingers while his left fingers curl ever more tightly around his sister's. And these are his write fingers too, grasping the pen he uses to describe this as he stares at the fingers of his left hand, open now and empty, his sister hundreds of miles away, his right fingers wrapped around his pen, grabbing hold, hanging on, full of these descriptions, while his left hand hangs at his side.

3.
'Take his hand,' they'd say, 'c'mon give him a hand.' 'It's very handy,' they'd add, by way of explanation, 'when the kids lend a hand, very touching,' they'd say, touching their eyes with their handkerchiefs. And if he couldn't grasp what they were saying, couldn't handle it, they'd put their fingers to their heads drawing circles with their fingertips, touch their fingers to their brows tapping them, as tho they were giving him the mental finger, as tho they were fingering him as mental. And everywhere he turned there were fingers: pointed at him as they shouted 'bang bang you're dead'; raised to ask questions, raised to answer them; stuck out to

signal this or that turn. Fingers like sharks as they wagged their jaws at him. Fins. GRRR.

4.
They put him in the front line in the touch football game. They put him in the front line in front of Moose. They put him in front of Moose whom noone else would stand in front of. They put him in the front line where he'd lean forward, balancing on his fingertips, as the Quarterback called the signals, as the ball was snapped, as Moose trampled over him rushing to follow the ball in. They put him in the front line and Moose trampled over him again and again, game after game, until the day his finger broke, snapped as he tried to touch Moose, as he tried to lay a hand on him, tried to carry out, somehow, the rules of the game. He wore a cast for weeks, covering his wrist and snaking out along his broken finger like a hook and when they asked what had happened, how had he broken his finger, he told them 'playing touch football'. And nobody laughed because nobody else would get in line in front of Moose. Noone else could or would touch him.

5.
The thing was he couldn't control his fingers properly. First there was the writing, making the O's so large they travelled above and below the blue lines in his copy book, beyond the red margin lay to the left of his pen. And he was told to get more control so he learned

to hold the pen funny, gripping it with three fingers as it rested on a fourth. And he learned to write small and tiny, learned to write between the lines, to leave so much white space around the writing that noone could read it. And they wanted him to write larger again and he couldn't. He could contain the fingers but he couldn't control them. Like later with the model plane kits— balsa wood, plastic—trying to make the bits fit, trying to be so careful, so precise, and he couldn't, wasn't, his fingers kept fumbling things, snapping them, clumsy in the attempt to apply decals, paint, glue, and he would finish these models, hold them up on his fingertips simulating flight, but they wouldn't, didn't, looked like they never had, never would, fly. They just sat there, on his fingers, on his shelf, making him feel guilty, useless, as if they were pointing the finger at him, at his failure, his inability to control his fingers.

6.
This is the way it went. He was to keep his sticky fingers off the dining room table. He was to keep his fingers to himself. He was not to finger himself (which made his fingers sticky), or her (which made his fingers sticky), or stick his finger in his nose (which made his fingers sticky). He was to keep them out of the cookie jar, off of the pie, on the handlebars, inside the car, around the golf club, above the table. But he was supposed to get a grip on himself, get a good grasp of languages, problems, situations, a good grasp on reality, be able

to reach people, touch them, get a feel for them, put his finger on the solution almost instantly. And you have to hand it to him, he handled the whole thing like a five finger exercise, kept his fingers on the pulse of the notion even when his reach exceeded his grasp, even when he was losing his grip, even when his head was whirling with more conflicting messages than you could count on the fingers of both hands, he handled them, he kept them in hand.

7.
First he was always trying to control his fingers. Later he learned the fingers controlled everything. Everyone thot in tens and had ten fingers (sort of) and when push came to shove anyone of them might be the one to push the big red button. Early on he learned the fingers gave you pleasure. You could feed yourself, play with yourself, finger things out, as you had to. Later he learned his fingers could give other people pleasure too, other fingers could give him pleasure, in the reaching, touching, evenhandedness of love. And when she married him, he took the ring that they had bought and placed it on her finger. And he cried. And she cried. And now he knew that finger had a real ring to it, there was something there, and maybe this was the first step in beginning to grasp it.

8.
What he wanted to do was play a musical instrument so he took up the violin. He took up the violin because they had one at school noone else wanted to play and they offered it to him, a real hand-me-down, offered him lessons and the violin and he went for it, got his hands on it and off he went. Except everyone at home hated it when he played it, hated it because he couldn't get the fingering right no matter how hard he tried, stood in the other room their fingers in their ringing ears as his fingers tried to wring the right sounds from the strings. And he couldn't, he didn't, he never will make that violin sing. Because he was all thumbs. Because his hands went haywire. Because his fingers fumbled it, his digits, dig it, didn't.

9.
After he had been writing for awhile he became aware of how many times he used the word 'fingers', the fact of them, the image of them, in his poems. All that talk of reaching and touching, all those barriers his fingers seemed to encounter between him and some imagined other. The metaphors. The similes. The symbolisms. And then one day he realized that of course he was always staring at his hand when he wrote, was always watching the pen as it moved along, gripped by his fingers, his fingers floating there in front of his eyes just above the words, above that single white sheet, just above these words i'm writing now, his fingers

between him and all that, like another person, a third person, when all along you thot it was just the two of you talking and he suddenly realized it was the three of them, handing it on from one to the other, his hand translating itself, his words slipping thru his fingers into the written world. You.

10.
Much later he began to write for puppets and there he was, day after day, watching his words come out of the mouths of fingers, watching hands turn to each other and say the lines he had spent so long struggling to perfect. And one day one of the hands turned to him and said: 'Hey, bp, what do you think?' And it had always been his fingers talking, his fingers shaping the letters, the words, that funny grip around the pen, the language, and he lifted his hand up, opening and closing his fingers, and said: 'Nothing.'

The Hips

1.
Not hip.

2.
Maw called them 'the Workman hips.' 'Too bad,' she'd say to me, 'you've got the Workman hips. Too bad,' she'd say to my sister, 'you've got the Workman hips. Too bad,' she'd say to my nieces, shaking her head in dismay, 'you've got the Workman hips,' she'd say, as generation after generation of family swayed past her on their way into history, 'you've got the Workman hips. Too bad,' she'd say.

3.
We tend not to think of them as different. We tend not to think of them as unique. We refer to them by direction—left or right—and when they're really wide we say 'hey, what a caboose,' as the hips sway away, left, then right, then left, disappearing in the distance. We tend to think of them distantly, something that's there where the body gets interesting, interested, and tho we say 'nice pair of hips,' its usually the waist, the way the bum shapes itself, the belly, the crotch, we're referring to. But then one day someone places their hand on your hip, lovingly, expectantly, and the hip they touch is different, unique, left or right, and it carries you away as they lay their hand there and you let it stay. You place your hand on their hip, press your bodies close together and say okay. Let the hips carry you away.

4.
I was just a kid. We were living in Port Arthur and it was Saturday afternoon and I had nothing else to do so I rode my bike down Oliver Road towards downtown and there was this big crowd gathered in an open field near a lumber yard and tables had been set up made of saw horses and spare lumber where you could buy juice and pop and there were booths with people in them selling things and people standing outside them buying things and I rode my bicycle into that field under the fluttering banners someone had strung

around it and there was a woman standing there in the middle of the crowd who had the biggest hips I'd ever seen. It turned out her name was Boxcar Annie or, at least, that's what the announcer said as I got off my bike, he said that we were about to see a log-chopping contest and Boxcar Annie, who was also called the Queen of the Hoboes and must've weighed at least 300 pounds, was the lone woman contestant. The idea was that each contestant had to chop a log clean thru and whoever finished first was the winner and he told them all to wait until he yelled go and he yelled go and I watched the whole contest, sweating man after burly sweating man and, of course, Boxcar Annie, who had the biggest hips I'd ever seen and will ever see, and Boxcar Annie beat every man in the place, beat them all easily, and everyone cheered and said how terrific Annie was, she really was the Queen of the Hoboes, and afterwards Annie went off to drink beer with the men she'd beaten and I got back on my bike and rode it all the way back up the hill to home. And I never have forgotten the sight of her, the way she chopped wood so effortlessly, precisely, rhythmically, chips flying, hips swaying, the biggest hips I've ever ever seen.

5.
It was because of my hips I started writing. I was in Grade 4. It was late fall or early spring, I can't remember which, but I remember the ditch, the one

near the school, and it was full of icy slush and a friend dared me to jump across it so I did. I remember leaping through the air and barely making it halfway across before my left foot, which was pointed down, began to enter the thick icy mixture of slush and water, my right leg still vainly reaching towards the far side of the ditch as my left leg followed my left foot down towards the untouched bottom, and I landed like some bad imitation of a ballet dancer, struck, my left leg burying itself in that slush right up to my hip, stuck, my right leg floating on the top. My hips kept me afloat. Or at least that's what the firemen said to my Maw when they brought me home after rescuing me. I'd been stuck in that freezing sludge for over an hour while my friend ran and told the teacher who phoned the fire department who came and laid ladders across on either side of me and pulled me up and out, and the firemen said that that ditch was so deep and the sludge so like quicksand I would've drowned if it hadn't been for the strange position of my legs and hips. And the cold I caught from being stuck in the ditch turned into bronchitis and they kept me home from school for over two weeks and during that time I wrote my first novel, The Sailor From Mars, all 26 chapters written by hand in a school copy book. It was all about a Martian sailor who came to Earth, went to work on a sailing ship and, along the way, fell in love with a girl called Luna who, I remember writing, 'was not of this world.' I can't remember now how the novel ended, or even how it went, and my Maw threw it away by mistake three years later so there's no way I can go back and refresh my memory, but I do remember that when I went back to school I showed it to my teacher and she read the whole thing to the class, a bit every morning for a week or two, just like a real serial, the kind I used to listen to all the time on the radio, and she said she liked it, and the kids said they liked it, and of course I loved it. I was alive and now I was a writer too. And really, when you get right down to it, you have to admit it was all thanks to my hips. And whenever people ask me 'how did you become a writer,' I always tend to say 'I just fell into it.' Right up to my hips. Believe me.

6.

Hip hip hooray, they'd say. Two hips, hooray? There had to be some meaning in it somewhere, some symbolism. Hip hip hooray, hip hip hooray, which meant someone had done something, outstanding, unique even, was okay. But later, when I was sixteen and in Grade 13 at King Eddy in Vancouver, I joined the Jazz Club and began to hang around jazz clubs with Sandy, whose brother was a jazz musician. And in all those clubs I went to—The Black Spot, Java Jazz, clubs that came and went and I can no longer attach a name to—in all those clubs I went to I learned it was not hip to shout hooray. It was not even hip to double the hip. It was only hip to be hip, single, unique, that was okay. So we sat there and said nothing except 'yeah' or 'hey' when the band was great, when the soloist was transported away in an improvisation we nodded, maybe grinned, tho even grinning was suspect in those days. Hip. Just hip. No hooray.

7.
You can never forget about your hips. My maw was always aware of her hips. She'd put on a dress and turn and look at herself in the mirror and sigh and you knew she was sighing about her hips. And even when they were invisible, like the time my Maw was in the hospital, the sheet pulled up to her waist, and the nurse came in and said 'my aren't you petite,' my Maw couldn't resist saying 'wait until you pull down this sheet,' because she couldn't forget about her hips. And now most days I feel this pain in my left hip, if I sit in a chair that isn't made just right, I feel this pain in my left hip, and I think about Maw, I think about Grandmaw, I wonder if all their lives too there was this nagging little pain saying I won't let you forget about me. And you don't let me forget about you do you? You're there reminding me, every time I stand too long, reminding me, every time the chair's too soft or too hard or too wrong. You're never going to let me forget about you. Are you hip?

The Anus

1.
It is an us—& yes we all have them. And as far as I can tell I never was able to see much difference between them. Just that little pucker among the cheeks. Whistle.

2.
My mother stuck a tube up it to give me an enema. I remember it was good for what ailed me. I remember it really cleaned me out. I remember lying over her knees with my pants down & her sticking this tube up me & me screaming 'THAT'S ENOUGH!' I remember thinking ma was the enema and the anus us. That's what confuse us say. Confuse us say an us don't make we we.

3.
We talked about it more than anything else down there. We didn't so much name it as allude to it. My maw said 'wherever you may be your winds blow free' or 'fox smells its own hole first.' My maw said 'whoever makes a smell like that must be rotten inside.' It was one of the big connections with the inside & thru it she knew whether you were sick or healthy & whether or not you needed an enema. You always looked to see if the things that came from it were firm or messy. You never referred to where they came from except to say the bum & to wonder, really, whether you had wiped it.

4.
When I read my first porno comic I found the word poot. People would be making love & fart & the sound effect read poot, poot, poot. Just the way the little engine that could said toot, toot, toot. Just like the joke about the fireman's big red fire engine going in & out of his wife's firehall. Hoot, hoot. Oot. I was trying to figure it oot.

5.
I came out of the movie with some friends & there was a christian recruiting group singing hymns across the street & this car drove by with this guy's ass stuck out the window hanging a moon for the world to see & the choir kept on singing just a closer walk with thee.

6.
The bum isn't the anus. The moon isn't green cheese. The last rose of summer is impossible to determine but when he drops it you know he's been there. Like my one brother hung a moon over my other brother's sleeping face. Then he dropped a rose that smelled like green cheese & my brother woke up yelling 'get your bum out of my face!'

7.
I just thot 'there's too many rhymes in this piece.' I just thot 'the anus rhymes both men & women.' I just thot about this guy I knew who after another guy raped him said 'he used me like a woman' & the woman I knew who was objecting to her lover's advances said 'he wanted to use me like a man.' I just thot about the anus & wrote down all I could. I just thot that the way I should end this piece is with the word 'anus' coz that's where a certain process in the body ends. I just thot that & now here I am writing this sentence's anus.

The Toes

1.
I was lying on my back on the grass in the park in front of our house staring at them & thot how ugly they looked. I was fifteen & really depressed & the clouds blew over the park & I stared at these two great clubs of flesh & bone with five little stubs sticking out of each of them & thot how ugly they looked & how maybe I should kill myself. I lay in the long grass beneath the oak trees & thot about killing myself & the ugliness of my toes & decided my suicide would have to be because of something else. This was the first time I ever really looked at my toes & boy were they something else. They were really ugly.

2.
In Port Arthur we went to the shoe section in the big department store where they had the free X-ray machine & shoved our feet into it & stared into the viewer & saw the bones in our toes moving. It was like the peepshow movieola we looked into at the sideshow where we always ran out of quarters just before we got to see the woman with all her clothes off but we saw our toes with all their flesh off & there were ten sets of bones we wiggled & there was no lead shielding & we did it almost every weekend for months. Maybe they mutated. Maybe they looked so ugly later because they'd mutated & it's all the fault of the shoe department in the big store whose name I no longer remember so there's nobody I can sue. Maybe this is the clue. Maybe postmodern writers like me all have post-atomic poetic feet & that's what makes them ugly to the pre-atomic eye & difficult to notate. Maybe this is THE ATTACK OF THE MUTANT POST-ATOMIC FEET! Maybe this is why we're always saying to the words: 'take me to your reader.'

3.
It was okay to talk about feet. It was okay to talk about toes. It was never okay to talk about toe-jam. If you talked about toe-jam you were really gross. I've never seen the word spelt before. I think I like it best just the way I've spelt it here, with the hyphen between the two words 'toe' & 'jam,' like the dark grungey hyphen

you were embarrassed to discover there, between your toes, inside your sock, your shoe, where you were never able to figure out how the toe-jam got.

4.
When Ellie & I moved in together we bought a house with six other people on Warren Road & the next door neighbours had a dog named 'toes.' It was like a sick joke & I felt fifteen again & the stupid dog chased me every time I walked from the house to the coach house & back again. It was like a bad dream where the repressed returns & there I was, toes yapping at me, toes jumping at me, toes trying to step on me, ugly & depressing & out to get me.

5.
I forget when I first noticed my toenails grew funny. Probably the same day I realized my feet were ugly. The big toenails were worst of all, flakey & fragmented, & the little toenails, almost non-existant, & the ones in between curling around the stubs of the toes, hugging them, so that even now, except for the big toe (which gets sharp & jagged & rips my socks), I don't have to cut them for months unless, of course, I feel like it. But it is easier if you keep them cut because of the dirt that wedges under them. And toenails are dull, like this paragraph, & in writing we're warned to cut the dull short. Except that no matter how short I cut them

they're still dull & lately I begin to think that maybe all you are saying when you say 'it's dull' is 'it's ugly & difficult to control'. And it really struck me the way the toenails curl around pressed flat against the stubby pink surfaces of the toes as tho they were hiding from me, fighting for their lives, feeding on the dirt & jam accumulation there, in the dark of the shoe, growing.

6.
Why were toes 'piggies'? Why did one of them go to market? When that last little piggie went 'wee-wee-wee,' how come he did it all the way home? We all know pigs become sausages & sausages look just like toes. Where do these metaphors & similes, these symbolisms, come from? Who makes up these resemblances, these languages, anyway? Why is it some days the words look so strange, so other, almost as if someone somewhere's speaking to me from behind them, thru them, trying to make me understand, instruct me, maybe even warn me—you know, trying to keep me on my toes?

The Lily

1.
They never called it by its real name. It was your wiener or your sausage. It was your thing. It dangled there between your legs & it was the real double entendre. It was your pencil or your other finger or your wee knee. It was everything but what it was and I looked down at it one day & suddenly realized, 'hey! that's what a pun is,' & it is.

2.
My mother was always telling me to shake it. It was only because I hadn't been circumcised. 'Be sure to shake your lily,' she'd say. It was a mixed metaphor but neither of us knew it. Neither of us knew that flowers were vaginas & that when I grew up hundreds

of women would be painting them. I stood there holding it in my hand as my mother yelled thru the door, 'don't forget to shake your lily son!' I'd make sure by shaking it harder than before.

3.
My father's was bigger. I'd see it when he walked from the bedroom to the bathroom in the middle of the night when I was supposed to be asleep. It wasn't traumatic. My dad looked too bleary as he staggered thru wearing only his pajama tops. Probably they'd just had sex. Years later I figured out probably my parents had just had sex coz dad's dick was just that little bit bigger, a real double extender. But back then I was always too busy trying to figure out what had happened to the bottom of his pajamas & whether he would make it to the bathroom before everything got too cold.

4.
When I was nine I joined the YMCA. I joined the YMCA because I wanted swimming lessons. I wanted swimming lessons but the YMCA wanted me to take them in the nude. It was 'optional' but all the instructors were really down on you if you were a 'poor sport' & wore your swimming trunks. So there we were, twenty nude nine-year old boys, & the instructors, in their swimming trunks, grinning at us

from the edge as we floundered in the water, & I went down gasping & came up, mouth open, right into this other boy's cock. I didn't want a mouthful of cock I wanted swimming lessons. 'But that's why everyone goes to the YMCA,' they said, and I said, 'no, all I want is swimming lessons.'

5.
When I rejoined the YMCA I kept noticing everyone's cock seemed bigger than mine. I was ten & thirteen-year-old-guys would strut around their cocks hanging down, or their towels draped in such a way you had to notice how big they were. Mine was small & at the least thing got even smaller. Like future man in Arthur C. Clarke's AGAINST THE FALL OF NIGHT. And I began to think that maybe I'd just evolved sooner than the rest & that was why everything would tuck up small & tiny into the body. Maybe I'd evolved a little sooner & maybe someday everybody would really admire the smooth streamlined look of my chopped & channelled cock. Yeah.

6.
The day I first masturbated was an accident. It was Easter & I was tossing in my sleep & I came. I came & then I came to & felt really bad. The sheets were sticky & my lily was drooping. Then the damn thing rose again. Even tho I thot holy thots it rose again,

& it was a lily & Easter & the symbolism was too confusing. The symbolism was too confusing & hadn't my mother told me to shake my lily? I shook my lily. How do you do? That?

Sum of the Parts

1.
So many things inside me I am not in touch with. So many things I depend on that I never see, pray I never see. As in the horror movie when the monster's taloned hand reaches in and pulls out your living spleen. So many things with such strange names. The sound of them is enough to make me vomit. And when I do, well, there it is, something from inside me, and I am in touch with it, can smell it, taste it, feel it, praying I'll never have to again, praying it will stop, the contraction in the throat, the sound from beyond the tongue, more in touch with my insides than I really wanted.

2.

If you're unlucky you get to meet them. If you're lucky you never get to meet them at all, they just nestle there, inside your body, monitoring, processing, producing, while you go about your life, oblivious. And this is the real organ music, the harmony of these spheres, the way the different organs play together, work, at that level beyond consciousness of which all consciousness is composed, the real unconscious, the unseen.

3.

It's the old problem of writing about something you know nothing about. I can do the research, read the books, but it's not the same. It's not the same. Tho they name the organs and the names are the same they're not the same organs as the organs sitting here inside me—the bpNichol liver, the bpNichol kidney, the bladder, pancreas, b p—collected working I think of as me. Which is why I worry if the doctor knows me, my work, when I go in, worry that that doctor may be a real collector, a completist. So you never ever say to the doctor, 'Doctor, please save me'. No, you never say that. You say, 'what's wrong with me?' or 'I'm in rotten shape!' or, even better, 'I'm worthless!', downplaying yourself, devaluing yourself, making yourself as miserable and undesirable as possible till the doctor says, 'Collect yourself!' And you do. And he doesn't. Which is how you want things to be.

4.
I almost got to meet my thyroid. I had been to see the Doctor and the Doctor said well it looked like my thyroid was enlarged and really I should get a thyroid scan and before you could say goiter there I was in this tiny room strapped down under this big machine & the technician was saying not to worry because nothing bad was going to happen, I only had to lie there as still as possible for fifteen minutes or so and then I could get up and leave. So I lay there, as still as possible, thinking about my thyroid, thinking about leaving, my nose itching, my throat dry, lay there aware of my thyroid, tho I couldn't see it, even tho I couldn't see the technician who even then was looking at it, pictures of it, aware of my unseen thyroid, aware of the unseen technician who had so carefully left the room after she had strapped me down under the big machine, who had so carefully closed the lead-shielded doors and told me not to worry. And of course I worried. I always worry. Even tho you say you'd like to see it, you always worry when there's a chance you might finally get your wish, might finally see it, the unseen, might finally enter into that world, like turning inside out, a raw feeling. See? No, you don't want to see.

5.
After I threw my back out I had more X-rays, X-rays of the lumbar sacrum region. Only the Doctor that

day was giving a lecture to these two trainees and as the technician shoved me around on the cold steel table he would whisper his commentaries. It was like those old T.V. game shows where the announcer would say 'what the studio audience doesn't know is,' and the trouble was I didn't know you see. You live your whole life making do with simply the names of your inner organs, their descriptions in books, while all around you are people who may actually have seen them, know directly what you only glimpse third-hand. Like your back. Every stranger on the street has had the chance to look at it but you only know it thru mirrors, photographs that other people take of you. And there are Doctors and Nurses who have cut you open, watched your blood flow, seen your heart pulse, know the inner man or woman. And these aren't just metaphors you know these aren't just similes. It is a discipline. We learn to see with the third eye, to listen with the third ear, to touch the unknown with the third hand, to walk down dark streets in search of the hidden, the unseen, while in the air around us invisible presences pick up their zithers and begin to play the Third Man Theme.

TECHNICAL DATA